John Rutter

Carols

10 carols for mixed voices

Contents

Index of Orchestrations 3

Angels' Carol 4
Candlelight Carol 13
Dormi, Jesu 18
Love came down at Christmas 25
Mary's Lullaby 28
Nativity Carol 33
Shepherd's Pipe Carol 37
Star Carol 46
There is a flower 53
What sweeter music 58

T0057098

MUSIC DEPARTMENT

OXFORD
UNIVERSITY PRESS

OXFORD
UNIVERSITY PRESS

Great Clarendon Street, Oxford OX2 6DP, England

Oxford University Press is a department of the University of Oxford.
It furthers the University's aim of excellence in research, scholarship,
and education by publishing worldwide

Oxford is a registered trade mark of Oxford University Press
in the UK and in certain other countries

This compilation © Oxford University Press 2005

The moral rights of the author have been asserted
Database right Oxford University Press (maker)

This collection first published 2005

All rights reserved. No part of this publication may be reproduced,
stored in a retrieval system, or transmitted, in any form or by any means,
without the prior permission in writing of Oxford University Press,
or as expressly permitted by law. Enquiries concerning reproduction
outside the scope of the above should be sent to the Music Copyright
Department, Oxford University Press, at the address above

Permission to perform the works in this anthology in public
(except in the course of divine worship) should normally be obtained
from the Performing Right Society Ltd. (PRS), 29/33 Berners Street,
London W1T 3AB, or its affiliated Societies in each country throughout
the world, unless the owner or the occupier of the premises
being used holds a licence from the Society

Permission to make a recording must be obtained in advance
from the Mechanical-Copyright Protection Society Ltd. (MCPS),
Elgar House, 41 Streatham High Road, London SW16 1ER,
or its affiliated Societies in each country throughout the world

16

ISBN 978-0-19-353381-3

Music originated on Sibelius
Printed in Great Britain on acid-free paper by
Halstan & Co. Ltd., Amersham, Bucks.

Cover photograph of John Rutter © Ian Cole

Index of Orchestrations

The accompanied items are all available in versions with orchestra. Full scores and instrumental parts are available on hire from the publisher, and also on sale where shown. In the USA some items are available from Hinshaw Music, Inc. Details of instrumentation are shown below.

Angels' Carol
2fl, ob, 2cl, bsn, 2hn, hp, str (*hire*)
In USA: available on sale from Hinshaw Music, Inc.

Candlelight Carol
fl, ob, hp, str (*hire*)
In USA: available on sale from Hinshaw Music, Inc.

Dormi, Jesu
strings (*hire*)
In USA: available on sale from Hinshaw Music, Inc.

Love came down at Christmas
strings (*hire*)

Mary's Lullaby
fl, ob, hp, str (*hire and sale*)

Nativity Carol
strings (and organ *ad lib.*) (*hire and sale*)

Shepherd's Pipe Carol
fl/picc, ob, bsn, 2hn, hp (opt), str (*hire and sale*)

Star Carol
2fl, 2ob, 2cl, 2bsn, 2hn, 2perc, hp, str (*hire and sale*)
Also available with brass accompaniment: 4tpt, 3tbn, tuba, timp, perc, piano or organ (*hire*)

What sweeter music
strings (*hire and sale*)

Hinshaw Music, Inc.: www.hinshawmusic.com

Angels' Carol

Words and music by
JOHN RUTTER

Also available separately (X325), and in a two-part version for upper voices (T117). In the USA, this four-part version is available separately from Hinshaw Music, Inc. (HMC1002); the two-part version is also available separately (HMC986).

© Oxford University Press 1988 and 2005. Photocopying this copyright material is ILLEGAL.

16
God that Christ the Lord is here?
19 A
SOPRANOS and TENORS
mf
Have you heard the news that they bring from hea - ven
23
(Sops. only)
To the hum-ble shep - herds who have wait - ed long?
(Tens. only)
cresc.
27
B
f joyfully
S. A. Glo-ri-a in ex - cel - sis De - o,
T. B. Glo - ri - a in ex - cel - sis,
B
f joyfully
f

30
mf
Glo-ri-a in ex-cel-sis De-o!
Hear the an-gels sing their joy-ful
Glo-ri-a in ex-cel-sis De-o!
mf
Hear them sing their joy-ful
mf
34
C
p
song.
Ah
unis.
p legato
song.
2. He is come in
C
dim.
p legato
38
Ah
peace in the win-ter's still-ness,
Like a gen-tle

42
Ah
mp
div.
snow - fall in the gen - tle night; He is come in
cresc.
46
mp cresc.
mf
Ah
Ah
mf dolce
joy like the sun at morn - ing Fill-ing all the
mf
50
Ah
D
dim.
p dolce
Ah
He is come in
dim.
world with ra - diance and with light.
D
dim.
p

54
love as the child of Ma - ry; In a sim - ple
p
Hum
58
sta - ble we have seen his birth:
poco cresc.
poco cresc.
poco cresc.
62
E
mp
Glo-ri - a in ex - cel - sis De - o!
mp
Glo-ri - a in ex - cel - sis De - o,
E
mp
dim.

66
p
Hear them sing 'Peace on earth'.
p
Hear the an - gels sing - ing 'Peace on earth'.
p
cresc.
mp cresc.
70
F
3. He will bring new light to a world in
f
f
3. He will bring new light to a world in
F
f
f
mf rhythmic
Ped.
sim.
74
dark - ness,
dark - ness, Like a bright star shin - ing in the skies a -

78
He will bring new hope
- bove;
He will bring new hope
He will bring new
He will bring new hope
81
— to the wait - ing na - - tions
When he comes to
to the na - - tions
hope
to the wait - ing na - - tions
— to the na - - - - - tions
84
reign in pu - ri - ty and love.
mf
mf
— When he comes in pu - ri - ty and love.
When he comes in love.
G
f
Let the earth re -
mf
When he comes in love.
f
G
mp
cresc.
mf

88
Let the earth re - joice at the Sa - viour's com - ing;
f
- joice at the Sa - viour's com - ing;
91
Let the hea - vens an - - swer with the joy - ful
Let the hea - vens an - - swer
Let the hea - vens an - - swer with the joy - ful
Let the hea - vens an - - swer
94
morn:
H
S. Glo - ri - a in ex -
with the joy - ful morn:
A. Glo - ri - a in ex -
morn:
with the morn:
T. B. Glo - - ri - a
H
cresc.
f

97
-cel - sis De - o,
-cel - sis De - o, Glo-ri - a in ex - cel - sis De - o!
in ex - cel - sis, Glo - - ri - a in ex - cel - sis!
dim.
100
mf
dim.
rall.
Hear the an - gels sing - ing 'Christ is born',
mf
Hear them sing - ing 'Christ is born',
dim.
rall.
mf
dim.
104
Tranquil ♩ = 92
p dolce
rall. al fine
S. A. Hear the an - gels sing - ing 'Christ is born'.
p
T. B. Hum
Tranquil ♩ = 92
rall. al fine
p
Ped.

for John Romeri and the Church of the Assumption, Pittsburgh

Candlelight Carol

Words and music by
JOHN RUTTER

Andante con moto ♩ = 92

Verse 1: SOPRANOS (and ALTOS)
Verse 2: TENORS (and BASSES)

VOICES

mp legato e dolce

1. How do you cap-ture the
2. Shep-herds and wise men will

ORGAN

Sw. *p legato*

Man.

Ped.

Ch.

Sw.

7(43)

wind on the wa - ter? How do you count all the stars in the
kneel and a - dore him, Se - ra - phim round him their vi - gil will

12(48)

cresc.

dim. *p*

sky? How can you mea - sure the love of a mo - ther, Or
keep; Na - tions pro - claim him their Lord and their Sa - viour, But

17(53)

how can you write down a ba - by's first cry?
Ma - ry will hold him and sing him to sleep.

Also available separately (X292) and in a version for SSAA (W104). In the USA this mixed-voice verson is available separately from Hinshaw Music, Inc. (HMC798); also available separately for SSAA (HMC894).

© Oxford University Press, 1985 and 2005. Photocopying this copyright material is ILLEGAL.

21(57)
p molto legato
cresc.
S.
Can-dle-light, an-gel light, fire - light and star - glow Shine on his
A.
Can - dle - light, an-gel light and star - glow Shine on his
T.
Can - dle - light, an-gel light and star - glow Shine on his
1
B.
Can - dle-light, an - gel light, fire - light and star - glow Shine on his
2
Can - dle - light, fire - light and star - glow Shine on his
Play in verse 2 only—verse 1 unaccompanied
Ch.
p
26(62)
f
cra - dle till break - ing of dawn. Glo-ri - a, glo- ri- a
cra - dle till break - ing of dawn. Glo - ri - a, glo - ri - a
cra - dle till break - ing of dawn. Glo - ri - a
cra - dle till break - ing of dawn. Glo - ri - a
cra - dle till break - ing of dawn. Glo - ri - a in
Play in both verses
Sw.
mf

31 (67)
dim.
mp
dim.
in ex-cel - sis De - o! An - gels are sing - ing; the Christ child is
in ex-cel-sis De - o! An - gels are sing - ing; the Christ child is
in ex-cel - sis De - o! An - gels are sing - ing; the Christ child is
in ex-cel-sis De - o! An - gels are sing - ing; the Christ child is
ex-cel - sis De - o! An - gels are sing - ing; the Christ child is
Ch.
p
36
1.
2.
S.
A.
born.
T.
B.
Man.
Ped.
73
3. Find him at Beth - le - hem laid in a

*or hum, at conductor's discretion

98
S.
Glo-ri- a, glo-ri- a in ex- cel - sis De- o!
A.
Glo - - - ri- a, glo - ri- a in ex-cel-sis De- o!
T.
dawn. Glo - - - ri - a in ex- cel - sis De - o!
1
dawn. Glo - ri - a in ex-cel-sis De - o!
B.
2
dawn. Glo - - ri - a in ex-cel - sis De - o!
Sw.
cresc.
f
dim.
103
rall.
mp
p
An - gels are sing - ing; the Christ child is born.
Hum
Ch.

for Stephen Cleobury and the choir of King's College, Cambridge

Dormi, Jesu

Words: Latin, origin unknown
English, S. T. Coleridge (1772–1834)

JOHN RUTTER

Also available separately (X433). In the USA, this carol is available separately from Hinshaw Music, Inc. (HMC1718).

© Oxford University Press 1999 and 2005. Photocopying this copyright material is ILLEGAL.

20
p
1
S.
Dor - mi Je - su, dor - mi Je - su, dor - mi Je - su
p
2
Dor - mi Je - su, dor - mi Je - su, dor - mi Je - su
pp molto legato
A.
Dor - - mi, dor - - mi, dor - mi Je - su
pp molto legato
T.
Dor - - mi, dor - mi Je - su, dor - mi Je - su
pp molto legato
1
B.
Dor - - mi, dor - - mi, dor - mi Je - su
pp molto legato
2
Dor - mi Je - su, dor - mi Je - su, dor - mi Je - su
26
mp
S.
blan - du - le: Dor - mi Je - su, dor - mi Je - su,
mp
blan - du - le: Dor - mi Je - su, dor - mi Je - su,
mp
A.
blan - du - le: Dor - mi Je - su, dor - mi Je - su,
mp
T.
blan - du - le: Dor - mi Je - su, dor - mi Je - su,
mp
B.
blan - du - le: Dor - mi Je - su, dor - mi Je - su,
mp
blan - du - le: Dor - mi Je - su, dor - mi Je - su,
mp
dim.
Ped.

32
S.
dor - mi Je - su blan - - du - le.
dor - mi Je - su blan - - du - le.
A.
dor - mi Je - su blan - - du - le.
T.
dor - mi Je - su blan - - du - le. 2. Si non dor-mis,
p dolce espress.
B.
dor - mi Je - su blan - - du - le. 2. Si non dor- mis,
p dolce espress.
dor - mi Je - su blan - - du - le. 2. Si non dor-mis,
p dolce espress.
(Ped.)
39
S.
A.
T.
ma - ter plo-rat In - ter fi - la can-tans o - rat, Blan - de, ve - ni,
mp
p
B.
ma - ter plo-rat In - ter fi - la can-tans o - rat, Blan - de, ve - ni,
mp
p

47
S.
pp
blan - de, ve - ni, som - nu - le.
A.
pp
blan - de, ve - ni, som - nu - le.
T.
pp
cresc.
mp
blan - de, ve - ni, som - nu - le. Dor - mi Je - su, dor - mi
B.
pp
cresc.
mp
blan - de, ve - ni, som - nu - le. Dor - mi Je - su, dor - mi
pp
cresc.
mp
Man.
Ped.
54
1
S.
2
mp
Dor - mi Je - su,
mp
Dor - mi Je - su,
A.
mp
Dor - mi Je - su,
T.
mp
Je - su, dor - mi Je - su blan - du - le: Dor - mi Je - su,
1
B.
2
mp
Je - su, dor - mi Je - su blan - du - le: Dor - mi Je - su,
mp
Je - su, dor - mi Je - su blan - du - le: Dor - mi Je - su,
p
mp

61
S.
dor - mi Je - su, dor - mi Je - su blan - - du - le.
A.
dor - mi Je - su, dor - mi Je - su blan - - du - le.
dor - mi Je - su, dor - mi Je - su blan - - du - le.
T.
dor - mi Je - su, dor - mi Je - su blan - - du - le.
B.
dor - mi Je - su, dor - mi Je - su blan - - du - le.
dor - mi Je - su, dor - mi Je - su blan - - du - le.
p
dim.
68
pp molto dolce
Sleep, sweet ba - by! my cares be - guil - ing: Mo - ther sits be - side thee,
Sleep, sweet ba - by! my cares be - guil - ing: Mo - ther sits be - side thee,
Sleep, sweet ba - by! my cares be - guil - ing: Mo - ther sits be - side thee,
Sleep, sweet ba - by! my cares be - guil - ing: Mo - ther sits be - side thee,

75
S.
smil - ing; Sleep, my dar-ling, sleep, my dar-ling, ten - der - ly.
A.
smil - ing; Sleep, my dar - ling, sleep, my dar - ling, ten - der - ly.
T.
smil - ing; Sleep, my dar - ling, sleep, my dar - ling, ten - der - ly.
B.
smil - ing; Sleep, my dar - ling, sleep, my dar - ling, ten - der - ly.
pp
82
poco rall.
p
1
S.
2
Dor - mi Je - su, dor - mi Je - su, dor - mi Je - su blan - du - le:
pp molto legato
A.
Dor - mi, dor - mi, dor - mi Je - su blan - du - le:
T.
Dor - mi, dor - mi Je - su, dor - mi Je - su blan - du - le:
B.
Dor - mi, dor - mi, dor - mi Je - su blan - du - le:
Dor - mi Je - su, dor - mi Je - su, dor - mi Je - su blan - du - le:
(Small notes optional)

90
un poco meno mosso ♪ = 80
mp
1
S.
Dor - mi Je - su, dor - mi Je - su, dor - mi Je - su blan -
2
Dor - mi Je - su, dor - mi Je - su, dor - mi Je - su blan -
A.
Dor - mi Je - su, dor - mi Je - su, dor - mi Je - su blan -
T.
Dor - mi Je - su, dor - mi Je - su, dor - mi Je - su blan -
B.
Dor - mi Je - su, dor - mi Je - su, dor - mi Je - su blan -
un poco meno mosso ♪ = 80
(Man.)
97
ritard.
a tempo
dim.
p
pp
ppp
- du - le, blan - du - le, Je - su.
- du - le, blan - du - le, dor - mi Je - su.
- du - le, blan - du - le, dor - mi Je - su.
- du - le, blan - du - le, dor - mi Je - su.
- du - le, blan - du - le, dor - mi Je - su.
- du - le, blan - du - le, dor - mi Je - su.
Ped.

Love came down at Christmas

Words by
Christina Rossetti (1830–94)

JOHN RUTTER

This carol may be performed in G flat major. Also available separately, in G flat major (X224).

© Oxford University Press 1971 and 2005. Photocopying this copyright material is ILLEGAL.

14
A
S.
A.
p
Ah
Ah
unis.
mp legato
T.
B.
2. Wor - ship we the God - head, Love in - car - nate,
A
(Ped.)
18
Ah
Ah
T. But where-with for
div.
mf
Love di-vine; Wor - ship we our Je - sus:
(p)
Ah
(Man.)
22
S. But where-with for sa - - cred sign?
(p)
sa - cred sign?
Ah
p
Ah
(Ped.)
(Man.)

26
B
p
3. Love shall be our to - ken, Love be yours and
p
B
(Man.)
30
cresc.
love be mine; Love to God and all men,
cresc.
33
mf
Love for plea and gift and sign; Love for plea and
mf
p
p
36
gift and sign.
poco rall.
gift and sign.
gift and sign.
gift and sign.
poco rall.
pp
(Ped.)

for JoAnne

Mary's Lullaby

Words and music by
JOHN RUTTER

Also available separately (X272), and in a version for SSA (W111).

© Oxford University Press 1979 and 2005. Photocopying this copyright material is ILLEGAL.

8(26)
sleep-ing: In a sta - ble cold and poor, Ox and ass their vi - gil
greet-ing: p 'Peace on earth, good-will to men.' Each to each the song re -
Hum
pp Aw
Hum
pp Aw
Hum
pp Aw
12(30)
p
keep - ing.
- peat - ing.
Sing lul - la - by, sing lul - la - by, my own dear son, my
p
Sing lul - la - by, lul - la - by, my own son, my
p
Sing lul - la - by, lul - la, my own, my
p
Sing lul - la - by, my own, my

16
child; Lul- la - by, sing lul - la - by; Lul- la - by, my lit - tle
pp
child; Lul - - - la - by, lul - la - by; Mm
pp
child; Lul - - - - la - - by; Mm
B.1 lu - - - la, lul - la - by;
pp
child; B.2 lul - - - la - - by; Mm
pp
pp
(Man.)
(Ped.)
1.
2.
20
ba - by.
ba - by.
1.
2.
p
(Man.)
(Man.)

TENORS
(with BARITONES ad lib.)
25
mp cantabile
3. Shep-herds kneel-ing by his bed Of-fer hom- age with-out mea-sure;
(Ped.)
30
S.
pp
Sing
A.
pp
Sing
T.
pp
Wise men, by a bright star led, Bring him gifts of rich-est trea-sure.
Sing
B.
pp
Sing

34
lul- la- by, sing lul- la- by, my own dear son, my child;
lul - la - by, lul- la - by, my own son, my child; Lul -
lul - la - by, lul - - - la, my own, my child; Lul -
lul - - - la - - by, my own, my child;
pp
(Man.)
38
Lul- la- by, sing lul- la- by; Lul- la- by, my lit- tle ba - by.
- - la - by, lul- la- by; Mm
- - la - by; Mm
B.1 lu - - - la, lul- la- by;
B.2 lul - - - la - by; Mm
pp
p
(Ped.)
rall.
42
espress.
pp

Nativity Carol

Words and music by
JOHN RUTTER

Also available separately (X169), and for unison voices (U154). A version for upper voices, SSA, is included in *Carols for Choirs 4*.

© Oxford University Press 1967 and 2005. Photocopying this copyright material is ILLEGAL.

21(77) sempre cresc.
pay;
f
dim.
aye,
Born_ to - day,_ your hom - age pay,_ For Christ_ is born_ for aye,_ Born_
sempre cresc.
pay;_
f Born_
dim.
for aye,
sempre cresc.
f
dim.
pp
28(84) Born_
pp
after v.3: cut to p. 35 for v.4
B
2. Cra-dled by mo-ther so fair,
p
on Christ - mas Day.
A.
T. Hum
B.
pp Born on
after v.3: cut to p. 35 for v.4
p
B
End of v.3: resume accomp.
(pp)
p
(Small notes for organ only)
35 Ten-der her lul - la - by; Ov - er her son_ so dear An - gel hosts
(p)

42
fill the sky.
Far a - way si - lent he lay, Born to -
pp
(A.T.B. half-open lips)
pp
pp
49
-day, your hom - age pay;
Christ is born for aye,
Born on
cresc.
mp
pp
cresc.
mp
pp
cresc.
mp
pp
56
Christ - mas Day.
C
(back to p. 33)
D
(from p. 34)
pp espress. e dolce
4. Love in that sta - ble was born In - to our hearts to
pp espress. e dolce
C
D
(from p. 34)
mp
pp Sw. strings

93
know. Far a -
p
flow; In - no - cent dream - ing babe, Make me thy love to know.
-way si - lent lay, To - day your hom - age
100
cresc. poco a poco
sempre cresc.
pp
Far a - way si - lent he lay, Born to - day, your hom - age
pp cresc. poco a poco
sempre cresc.
cresc. poco a poco
sempre cresc.
107
f
mp
pp
rit.
pay; Christ is born for aye, Born on Christ - mas Day.
mp
f
pp
rit.
mf
p
pp

Shepherd's Pipe Carol

Words and music by
JOHN RUTTER

Also available separately (X167), and in versions for SSAA (W76), and for unison voices (U133).

© Oxford University Press 1967 and 2005. Photocopying this copyright material is ILLEGAL.

10
p
shep-herd boy pi - ping On the way to Beth - le-hem,
hills so lone - ly
p
A
13
S. An - gels in the sky brought this mes - sage nigh:
mf
legato
A. T. B. An - gels brought this mes - sage: 'Dance and sing for joy that
mf legato
mf
18
new-born King is
dim.
Christ the King is come to bring us peace on earth, and he's ly - ing
dim.
mp
dim.

22
p non stacc.
1.
2.
B
cra - dled there at Beth - le - hem.'
p non stacc.
p
mf
p
Ped.
Ped.
26
C
mp dolce e legato
S.
3. 'None may hear my pipes on these hills so lone - ly
A.
p
Ah
T.
p
Ah
B.
p
Ah
C

29
On the way to Beth - le - hem;
But a King will hear me
Ah
Ah
Ah
Ah
Ah
32
play sweet lul - la - bies When I get to Beth - le - hem.'
cresc.
Ah
Ah
Ah
35
D
mp
Ah
(mp)
Hov - ered o'er the man - ger
mp
Ah
dim.
p
mf legato
An - gels in the sky came down from on high,
Ah
p
mp
Ah
dim.
Ah
p
8va
p

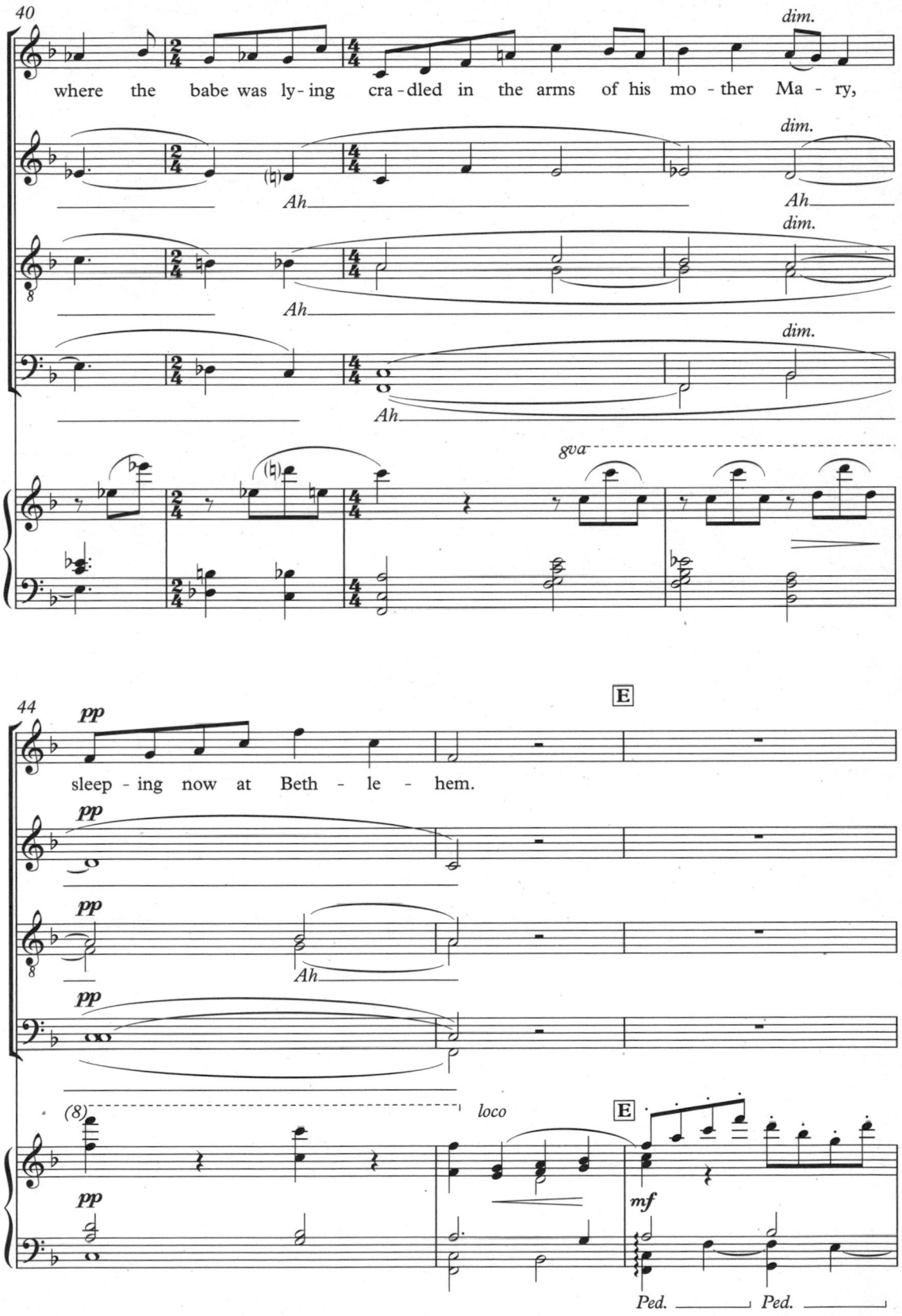
40
dim.
where the babe was ly-ing cra-dled in the arms of his mo-ther Ma-ry,
Ah
8va
44
pp
E
sleep-ing now at Beth-le-hem.
(8)
loco
mf
Ped.

47
TENORS and BASSES
mf crisply
4. 'Where is this new King, shep-herd boy pi-ping-mer-ri-ly,
8va
tr
mp
50
mp
Is he there at Beth - le - hem?'
mf
'I will find him soon by the
mp
(8)
tr
Ped.
53
star shi-ning bright - ly
In the sky o'er Beth - le - hem.'
mf
(8)
tr
loco

56
An - gels in the sky brought this mes - sage nigh:
f
An - gels brought this mes - - sage: Dance and sing for
f
gva
f
60
new - born King is
joy that Christ the King is come to bring us peace on
(8)
tr
mf
64
dim.
mp
earth, and he's ly - ing cra - dled there at Beth - le - hem.'
dim.
mp
(8)
tr
dim.
mp
mf

F
67
mf
5. 'May I come with you, shep-herd boy pi-ping mer-ri-ly, Come with you to Beth-le-hem?
mf
legato
mp
70
Pay my hom-age too at the new King's cra-dle,
mf
73
Is it far to Beth-le-hem?'
G
An-gels in the sky
f
An-gels
f
mp
6
f

76
brought this mes - sage nigh:
brought this mes - sage: 'Dance and sing for joy that Christ the
8va
81
in - fant King is
dim.
King is born this night in low - ly sta - ble yon - der,
dim.
mf
mp
84
H
p
rit.
Born for you at Beth - - - le - hem.'
p
H
8va
rit.
p
ff

for Sir David Willcocks and The Bach Choir

Star Carol

Words and music by
JOHN RUTTER

Also available separately (X233), and in a version for unison voices (U153).

© Oxford University Press 1972 and 2005. Photocopying this copyright material is ILLEGAL.

*Children and/or audience may join in the melody of the refrain, which can be taught at the time of the performance.

*or hum, at conductor's discretion

50
lov - ing arms a - sleep. Shep - herds poor, come to wor - ship and a - dore him,
Ah
Ah
Ah
Ah
Ah
53
Of - fer their hum - ble gifts be - fore the son of Ma - ry.
S.
A.
Ah
Ah
T.
B.
p
D
57
p legato
See his star shin - ing bright In the sky this Christ - mas Night! Fol - low me
p legato
D

62
joy - ful - ly; Hur - ry to Beth - le - hem and see the son of Ma - ry!
mf
66
E
f
4. Let us all pay our hom-age at the man - ger,
f
E
f
70
Sing his praise on this joy - ful Christ-mas Night; Christ is come, bring - ing

73
mf
pro - mise of sal - va - tion; Hur - ry to Beth - le - hem and see the son of
mf
mf
76
F
f
Ma - ry! See his star shin - ing bright
f
F
cresc.
f
Ped. sim.
80
In the sky this Christ - mas Night! Fol - low me joy - ful - ly;

84
G
mf
cresc.
Hur - ry to Beth - le - hem and see the son of Ma - ry,
mf
cresc.
G
mf

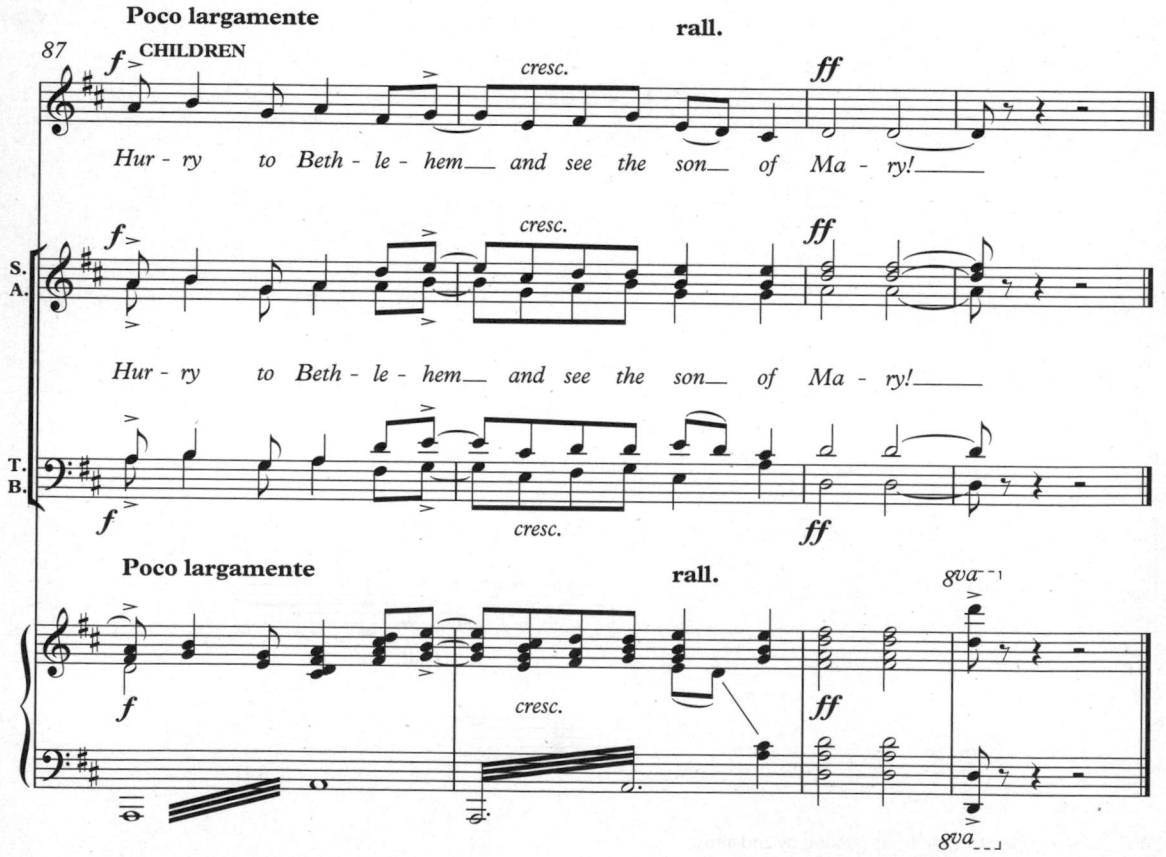
Poco largamente
rall.
87
f
CHILDREN
cresc.
ff
Hur - ry to Beth - le - hem and see the son of Ma - ry!
S.
A.
f
cresc.
ff
Hur - ry to Beth - le - hem and see the son of Ma - ry!
T.
B.
f
cresc.
ff
Poco largamente
rall.
8va
f
cresc.
ff
8va

for Dr George Guest and the choir of St John's College, Cambridge

There is a flower

Words by
John Audelay (15th century)

JOHN RUTTER

*Alternatively, these three bars may be sung by 2nd altos.

Also available separately (X295)

© Oxford University Press 1986 and 2005. Photocopying this copyright material is ILLEGAL.

*sand = gift

†Alternatively, the choir 1 part may be sung by solo tenor in verse 2 and solo soprano in verse 3.

44
blos - som
mp
mf
blos - som be - gan to *bed, Then rich and poor of ev - 'ry
blos - som
47
S.
land They mar-velled how this flow'r might spread.
A.
land Mar-velled how this flow'r might spread.
T.
(mf)
land Mar-velled how this flow'r might spread, Till king - es
B.
div. (mf)
land Mar-velled how this flow'r might spread, Till king - es
Poco più mosso ♩ = c. 69
50
1
S.
Al - le - lu - ia,
2
(2nd SOPRANOS) mp
Al - le - lu - ia,
A.
Al - le - lu - ia, al - le -
T.
dim.
three That bless - ed flo - wer came to see.
5. An - gels there
B.
dim.
three came to see.
5. An - gels there

*bed = bud

54
cresc.
mf
cresc.
al - le - lu - ia, al - le - lu - ia, al - le - lu - ia,
cresc.
mf
cresc.
f
al - le - lu - ia, al - le - lu - ia, al - le - lu - ia, al - le -
cresc.
mf
-lu - ia, al - le - lu - ia, al - le - lu - ia, al - le - lu - ia,
f
came from hea - ven's tower To look up - on this fresh - e - le
f
came from hea - ven's tower To look up - on this fresh - e - le

57
f
mf
rall.
mp
al - le - lu - ia, al - le - lu - ia, al - le - lu - ia, al - le - lu - ia, al - le -
-lu - ia, al - le - lu - ia, al - le - lu - ia, al - le - lu - ia, al - le - lu - ia, al - le -
f
mf
mp
al - le - lu - ia, al - le - lu - ia, al - le - lu - ia, al - le - lu - ia, al - le -
mf
dim.
flow'r, How fair he was in his co - lour And how sweet in his sa -
mf
dim.
flow'r, How fair he was in his co - lour And how sweet in his sa -

61
Tempo I ♩ = c.63
p dolce
- lu - ia. And to be - hold How such a flow'r might spring in
- lu - ia. And to be - hold How such a flow'r might spring in
- lu - ia. And to be - hold How such a flow'r might spring in
-vour; And to be - hold How such a flow'r might spring in
-vour; And to be - hold How such a flow'r might spring in
64
SOPRANO SOLO
mp
There is a flow'r sprung of a tree, The root there - of is call - èd Jes-
poco cresc.
S.
A.
gold.
dim.
p
gold. Hum
T.
B.
68
mf
-se, A flow'r of price; There is none such in pa - ra - dise.
dim.
rall.
mp
pp
(Hum)

for Stephen Cleobury and
the choir of King's College, Cambridge

What sweeter music

*Words by
Robert Herrick
(1591–1674)

JOHN RUTTER

*Slightly abridged and altered

Also available separately (X319)

© Oxford University Press 1988 and 2005. Photocopying this copyright material is ILLEGAL.

poco meno mosso
dim.
14
T.
B.
-way, And give the ho - nour to this day That sees De - cem - ber turn'd to
dim.
poco rit.
a tempo ♩ = 66
18
S.
A.
pp
That sees De - cem - ber turn'd to May.
p
pp
mp cantabile
unis.
T.
B.
May,
Why does the chill - ing win - ter's
poco rit.
a tempo ♩ = 66
p
mp
Ped.
22
T.
B.
mf
morn Smile, like a field be - set with corn? Or smell like a mea - dow new - ly
mf
f dolce
mp
26
shorn Thus on the sud - den? Come and see The cause, why things thus fra - grant
mp

30
SOPRANOS
div.
mp
mf
'Tis he is born, whose quick-'ning birth Gives life and lu - stre, pub-lic
ALTOS
mp
mf
'Tis he is born, whose quick-'ning birth Gives life and lu - stre, pub-lic
T.
B.
be:
Fl.
Man.
(Man.)
34
S.
mp
p molto legato
unis.
mirth, To hea-ven and the un-der-earth. We see him come, and know him
A.
mp
p molto legato
mirth, To hea-ven and the un-der-earth. We see him come, and know him
T.
p molto legato
We see him come, and know him
B.
p molto legato
We see him come, and know him
p
(Organ tacet)

38
mp
ours, Who, with his sun-shine and his show'rs, Turns all the pa - tient ground to
ours, Who, with his sun-shine and his show'rs, Turns the pa - tient ground to
ours, Who, with his sun-shine and his show'rs, Turns the pa - tient ground to
ours, Who, with his sun-shine and his show'rs,
42
mf
p
flow'rs, turns all the pa - tient ground to flow'rs. The dar-ling of the
flow'rs, turns all the pa - tient ground to flow'rs. The dar-ling of the
pp
flow'rs, turns all the pa - tient ground to flow'rs. The dar - ling of the
mp
turns all the ground to flow'rs.
46
S.
unis.
world is come, And fit it is, we find a room To wel-come him, to
A.
world is come, And fit it is, we find a room To wel-come him, to
T.
(pp)
world is come, we find a room to
pp
Man.

50
S.
wel-come him.
Which we will
A.
wel-come him.
Which we will
T.
wel-come him. The no-bler part of all the house here, is the heart, Which we will
B.
The no-bler part of all the house here, is the heart, Which we will
mp
cresc.
mf
Ped.
54
give him; and be-queath This hol-ly, and this i-vy wreath,
give him; and be-queath This hol-ly, and this i-vy wreath,
give him; and be-queath This hol-ly, and this i-vy wreath, To do him
give him; and be-queath this hol-ly, and this i-vy wreath, To do him
p

58
ALTOS
mf
poco f
mf
p
And Lord of all this re - vel - ling.
ho - nour; who's our King, And Lord of all this re - vel - ling.
ho - nour; who's our King, And Lord of all this re - vel - ling.
62
pp molto dolce
unis.
What sweet - er mu - sic can we bring Than a
(Ped.)
66
mp
poco rit.
ca - rol, for to sing The birth of this our heav'n - ly

69
poco meno mosso
rit.
S.
p
dim.
King, the birth of this our hea - ven - ly
A.
p
dim.
King.
(Hum)
T.
p
dim.
King.
(Hum)
B.
p
div.
dim.
King.
(Hum)
poco meno mosso
rit.
dim.
72
a tempo
rit.
pp
King.
pp
pp
pp
a tempo
rit.
pp
(Ped.)